IT'S MY STATE! ★

MISSISSIPPI

Ann Graham Gaines

Cavendish Square

New York

Published in 2014 by Cavendish Square Publishing, LLC
303 Park Avenue South, Suite 1247, New York, NY 10010

Library of Congress Cataloging-in-Publication Data

Gaines, Ann.
 Mississippi / Ann Graham Gaines. — [Second edition].
    pages cm. — (It's my state)
 Includes index.
 ISBN 978-1-62712-239-9 (hardcover) — ISBN 978-1-62712-492-8 (paperback) ISBN 978-1-62712-250-4 (ebook)
 1. Mississippi—Juvenile literature. I. Title.

 F341.3.G35 2014
 976.2—dc23

                    2013033720

This edition developed for Cavendish Square Publishing by RJF Publishing LLC (www.RJFpublishing.com)
Series Designer, Second Edition: Tammy West/Westgraphix LLC
Editorial Director: Dean Miller
Editor: Sara Howell
Copy Editor: Cynthia Roby
Art Director: Jeffrey Talbot
Layout Design: Erica Clendening
Production Manager: Jennifer Ryder-Talbot

MISSISSIPPI

CONTENTS

THE MAGNOLIA STATE

A Quick Look at
MISSISSIPPI

State Flower: Magnolia

In 1900, the magnolia blossom was voted in as state flower by Mississippi's schoolchildren. Students voted again in the early 1930s for their favorite tree. Once more, the magnolia came out on top. Wild magnolia trees can grow to be 60 feet (18 m) or more. Their heavily scented flowers, which blossom in the spring, come in white and cream.

State Bird: Mockingbird

The gray and white mockingbird, which is seen all over Mississippi, is a loud and energetic singer. The bird mimics other birds' songs, and that is why "mocking" is part of its name.

State Insect: Honeybee

Honeybees were designated as Mississippi's state insect in 1980. The honey they produce is often sold in Mississippi at farmers markets and roadside stands.

State Water Mammal: Bottlenose Dolphin

Not every state has an official water mammal but Mississippi does. The bottlenose dolphin, also called a porpoise, lives off the coast of Mississippi in the deep waters of the Gulf of Mexico. A member of the whale family, the bottlenose has sharp teeth, a small snout, and a dorsal fin on its back. It breathes through a blowhole located on top of its head. Dolphins are social creatures and live and travel in groups called pods.

State Fossil: Prehistoric Whale

Fifty million years ago, Mississippi was covered by an ocean that was filled with life. One of the most amazing creatures to swim in those waters was the prehistoric whale, also known as the Basilosaurus. This creature could grow to be 80 feet (24.4 m) long. It had vertebrae (individual bones in its spine) that were more than 1 foot (0.3 m) long. In 1981, the Mississippi state government declared the prehistoric whale as the official state fossil.

State Shell: Oyster Shell

Oyster shells were made the state shell in 1974. Oysters, which live in saltwater, are a valuable part of the Gulf Coast fishing industry. However, over the last decade, the oyster industry has been threatened by hurricanes, oil spills, and large amounts of freshwater from spillways designed to protect cities from flooding.

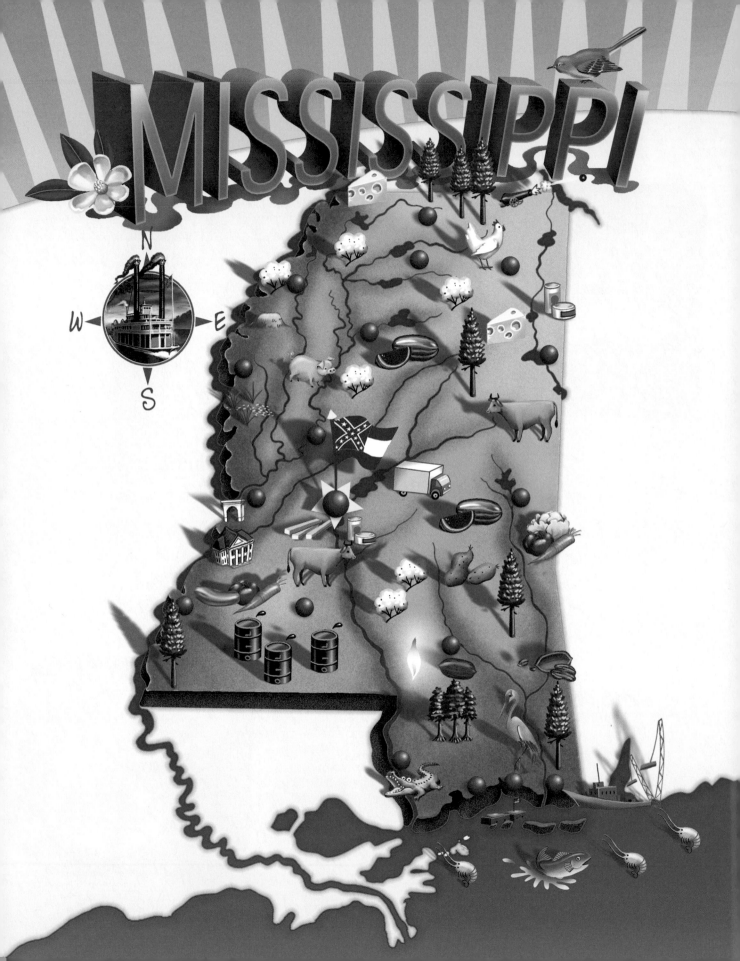

MISSISSIPPI

N
W · E
S

The Magnolia State

Charley Pride, a famous country singer and member of the Grand Ole Opry, was born in the town of Sledge, in Mississippi. He once said of his home state, "I loved Mississippi and do to this day. The rainbows that stretch from horizon to horizon after a summer rain are the most spectacular I have ever seen." For a small state—just thirty-second in size compared with other US states—Mississippi's landscapes are spectacular. The state runs about 350 miles (563 km) from north to south and 140 miles (225 km) from east to west. Within those 48,282 square miles (125,050 sq km) are rolling hills, slow-moving waterways called bayous, rushing streams, large and small rivers, farmland, sleepy towns, and several bustling cities.

Mississippi's Location

Situated on the Gulf of Mexico, Mississippi is a part of the United States that geographers call the Deep South. In terms of both geography and way of life, the state is often grouped with Louisiana, which sits to the west, and Alabama and Georgia, to the east.

Quick Facts

Mississippi's Borders

North	Tennessee
South	Louisiana
	Gulf of Mexico
East	Alabama
West	Louisiana
	Arkansas
	Mississippi River

Satellite images of the Mississippi River, such as this one taken in 2001, track the constant changes the river makes in the delta.

Mississippi's shape looks much like a rectangle. The Mississippi River forms the state's western boundary. As the river weaves in and out, so does the state's western border. Louisiana cuts a small notch into Mississippi's rectangular shape.

A Rich Land

Three important physical features shaped Mississippi's landscape. The first is the Appalachian Mountains, a long mountain chain that runs along the United States' eastern seaboard. One peak of the Appalachians, called Woodall Mountain, rises 806 feet (246 m) above sea level. This is Mississippi's highest point.

Rain that falls on these Mississippi River headwaters in Minnesota takes 90 days to reach Mississippi.

An even greater influence than the Appalachians on Mississippi's land is its major river. The Mississippi River begins as a narrow stream, just 20 to 30 feet (6–9 m) wide, up north in Minnesota. By the time its waters reach the state of Mississippi, over 400 miles (644 km) later, the river is 2 miles (3.2 km) wide in some parts. For thousands of years, the river's ever-changing waters have built up a broad, flat delta in the western part of Mississippi. Also called an alluvial plain, the delta is an area where the river's floodwaters have deposited a thick layer of rich, black soil over the land.

The Vicksburg bridge, seen on the left, was built across the MIssissippi River in 1973. It stands next to the Old Vicksburg Bridge, seen on the right, which was built in 1930 and today carries trains across the wide river.

The Mississippi River has also created special water features called oxbow lakes. Many of these lakes formed naturally over long periods of time. As loops of the river became cut off from the rest of the river, they formed small, U-shaped lakes. Other oxbow lakes have formed when engineers reshaped the river with dams to control flooding.

To the south of the state lies the Gulf of Mexico. Measured in a straight line, Mississippi's coastline is 40 miles (64 km) long. However, its coastline is anything but straight. Many bays and coves cut into the land along the southern coastline.

If you followed all the ins and outs of these inlets, you would discover that the shoreline actually measures around 350 miles (563 km). Pounded by waves in many places, the shape of the coastline shifts constantly. A chain of small islands along the shore offers some protection for the mainland from storms that the Gulf blows in.

Mississippi's Waters

Abundant waterways make Mississippi a very green state. Rivers of all sizes flow across the land. While the Mississippi River is the state's largest river, it is just one of many. The state also has numerous bayous. These marshy streams move so slowly, they hardly seem to move at all. Some bayous connect lakes and rivers in what is called the Delta Region of the state. Other bayous to the south empty into inland waters and then into the Gulf of Mexico.

Through the western part of the state flow tributaries. These are other rivers from which waters eventually empty into the Mississippi River. These tributaries include the Yalobusha and Tallahatchie rivers, which meet just north of the city of Greenwood, and form a single river, called the Yazoo. This important waterway runs south and west until it reaches the city of Vicksburg and the Mississippi River. Running a similar course, the Big Black River crosses the state from east to west before emptying into the Mississippi River.

The central and eastern parts of the state are covered by smaller rivers and creeks that grow in size as they run south toward the Gulf of Mexico. These include the Pascagoula and the Chickasawhay rivers as well as the much larger Pearl River.

In the northeastern part of the state, the Tombigbee River runs south into Alabama, where it continues its course to the Gulf of Mexico.

Mississippi has many lakes, the largest of which have been created by damming rivers. Among such bodies of water are the Ross Barnett Reservoir on the Pearl River; Arkabutla Lake on the Coldwater River; Grenada Lake on the Yalobusha River; and the Pickwick Lake on the Tennessee River.

The Delta Region

Some geographers divide the state into two regions: the Alluvial Plain, or Delta, to the west, and the East Gulf Coastal Plain. However, Mississippians usually think of their state as having five distinct regions: the Delta Region, the Capital/ River Region, the Hills Region, the Pines Region, and the Coastal Region.

The Delta Region is located between the Mississippi and the Yazoo rivers. This flat area frequently floods and spreads a kind of soil called silt along the way. Rich soil in an area called the Bottomlands supports huge trees, luscious plants and vines, and many of Mississippi's agricultural crops. Outcroppings, called bluffs, rise from the riverbanks in parts of the Delta Region where the Mississippi River has cut a path over time.

Paddle wheelers, steamboats, barges, and freighters replaced the dugout canoes that Native Americans once used to travel along the Mississippi River.

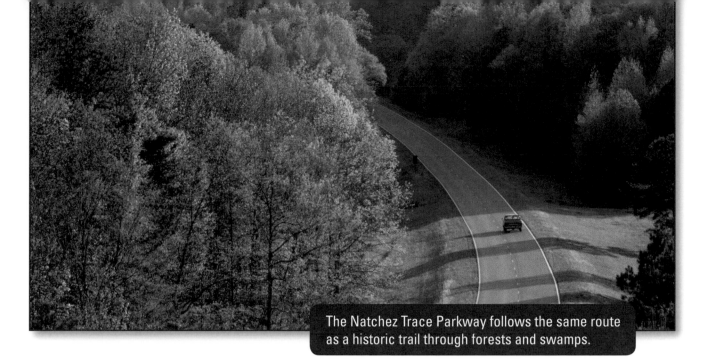

The Natchez Trace Parkway follows the same route as a historic trail through forests and swamps.

The Capital/River Region

Mississippians tend to refer to the southwestern corner of their state as the Capital/River Region. The area, bound by the Mississippi River on the west and the Pearl River on the east, stretches south to the dividing line between Mississippi and Louisiana. The cities of Vicksburg and Jackson are on the northern border of the area. The Capital/River Region looks much like the Delta Region, with river bluffs, flatland, and many bayous and oxbow lakes. However, the Capital/River Region is much more heavily populated.

One population center of the region is Jackson. It is not only the state's capital but also Mississippi's largest city. Suburbs and small towns have grown up around Jackson. Parts of the region look like places all across the United States, with housing developments, strip malls, and parking lots. Not all of the construction in this area is modern, however. In some parts of Jackson, historical Southern architecture has been preserved.

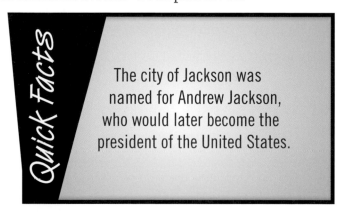

Quick Facts

The city of Jackson was named for Andrew Jackson, who would later become the president of the United States.

The Hills Region

In the northeastern part of the state is a hilly section called the Hills Region. In the extreme northeastern corner of the Hills Region are the sandy Tennessee River Hills. To the west, in the center of this area, is Pontotoc Ridge. The Appalachian Mountains begin their rise in the north, into Tennessee. Much of this part of the Hills Region is wooded. The federal government established two national forests here. Some of the towns in this region are Corinth, Oxford, and Tupelo, the birthplace of Elvis Presley.

> ## *In Their Own Words*
>
> *In several sections, both natural in the banks of the Mississippi and its numerous arms, and where artificial canals had been cut, I observed erect stumps, with their roots attached, buried in strata at different heights, one over the other.*
>
> —Charles Lyell, geologist, in 1863

The Pines

Early explorers describe the area that is now Mississippi as a forested land. Today a broad band of piney woods cuts across the center of the state, which Mississippians call the Pines Region. This area stretches from the Hills Region up to the coastal plain. Lumbering and farming centers lie in cleared areas of these forests. Like the Delta to its west and the Hills to its north, this region is sparsely populated.

The Coastal Region

To the south of the Pines Region is the Coastal Region along the Gulf of Mexico. A string of islands lies offshore in the Gulf of Mexico. In 1969, Hurricane Camille split Ship Island in two. One half of the former island is now called East Ship Island. It is a place where ships have anchored ever since the British Navy stayed there during the War of 1812.

The part of the Gulf that lies between these coastal islands and the rest of the state is called the Mississippi Sound, a long and shallow body of water. There are large bays at the towns of Bay St. Louis and Pascagoula. As the Pearl and Pascagoula rivers flow into the sound, they form wide deltas with marshes and swampland.

In this region are the old port cities of Biloxi, Gulfport, Pascagoula, and Bienville. Visitors flock to the white beaches along Mississippi's shoreline with its many resorts and campgrounds. Just up from the coast, a series of sand steps or terraces have formed from sand that blows in from the Gulf.

Many people worked hard to clean the beaches along the Gulf coast that had been affected by the 2010 oil spill.

Climate

Mississippi's rivers, lakes, bayous, ocean, and warm climate make it a hot, humid place for much of the year. Temperatures seldom dip below 40°F (4.4°C) in the winter, but reach an average of around 92°F (33.3°C) in the summer.

Hurricanes regularly threaten the state, especially along its Gulf Coast. Hurricane Camille hit Mississippi hard in 1969. However, even people who survived Camille agree that Hurricane Katrina hit harder when it roared into Mississippi on August 29, 2005. Winds measured 145 miles per hour (233 km/h) when Katrina made landfall in Louisiana. That made it one of the strongest hurricanes ever to hit the United States. After making landfall, the hurricane skipped along the shore a little farther east. It came ashore for a second time, this time at the Louisiana/Mississippi border. The winds had decreased a little, but they still measured 125 miles per hour (201 km/h). Not only did the wind cause great damage, but so did a huge storm surge. This powerful moving wall of water rushed into Mississippi's coastal cities. Most of the buildings along the shore were wiped out or heavily damaged. One storm surge near the town of Pass Christian measured 27.8 feet (8.5 m), making it the largest ever recorded in the United States. Katrina's winds and storm surges also caused great damage to Waveland, Bay St. Louis, Long Beach, Gulfport, Ocean Springs, Gautier, and Pascagoula.

In addition to the devastating hurricane, 11 tornadoes accompanied Katrina in Mississippi. Two of them were rated as F2 on the Fujita Scale. That means the tornadoes caused significant damage and packed winds of anywhere between 113 and 157 miles per hour (182–253 km/h).

The remains of this home in Biloxi show some of the damage caused in the state by Hurricane Katrina.

When the storm had passed, more than 200 people in Mississippi had been killed and thousands of homes and businesses had been destroyed. Affected families had to find temporary places to live in shelters, trailers, and in the homes of relatives or even strangers who lived in safer areas. When President George W. Bush toured the state in May 2006, he expressed admiration for the people of the state who were working hard to rebuild. He said that Mississippians showed "a strength that wind and water can never take away."

Each year brings the possibility of hurricanes and tornadoes to the state. However, the people of Mississippi continue to come up with new ways to protect themselves from danger. For example, after Hurricane Katrina, buildings and bridges were rebuilt to be stronger than they were before. The emergency command centers along the coast had been flooded during the storm, so they were rebuilt on higher ground. A new coastal Mississippi is on the way!

Red-cockaded woodpeckers make their homes in pine forests. They eat mostly ants, caterpillars, spiders, and berries.

Mississippi's Wild Places

In a state where over half the land is covered with forest, there is something for every nature lover. The forested areas are filled with a wide variety of trees, wildlife, and wildflowers.

The northern forests of Mississippi support hardwoods, including elm, hickory, and oak, as well as evergreens. The town of Tupelo is named after a special gum tree that flourishes in swamps and other wet places. Several kinds of pine trees—the longleaf, slash pine, and loblolly—grow mainly in the south.

White-tailed deer live all across the state, often moving out from the forests into populated areas. Mississippi's forests and fields are also home to wild hogs, black bears, squirrels, foxes, opossums, rabbits, raccoons, and skunks.

Mississippi's forests shelter a variety of birds, such as eastern wild turkeys, bobwhite quail, mourning doves, and woodcocks. Birdwatchers thrill at the sight of the red-cockaded woodpecker, a bird that is on the rare and endangered species list.

Black-eyed Susans bloom from June to October. The plants were often used by Native Americans to make medicines.

Mississippi's wildflowers and tree blossoms burst into color in the spring. These flowers include pink and red wild azaleas, creamy magnolias, black-eyed Susans, pale pink camellias, purple and white iris, pink and white dogwood blossoms, violets; tiny trillium flowers in whites, yellows, and reds, and the ivory Cherokee rose, which Native Americans first cultivated in the area.

Mississippi's wild wetlands also shelter large numbers of animals and birds. Millions of water birds such as ducks, geese, and swans live in rivers, streams, and bayous. Egrets, herons, and terns nest along the coastal shorelines and the banks of Mississippi's rivers and lakes. Alligators, snapping turtles, and water snakes, including the venomous, or poisonous, cottonmouth, populate the state's waterways. Bass, bream, catfish, croaker, and perch swim in Mississippi's fresh waters. Other creatures found in coastal waters include saltwater fish such as mackerel, menhaden, and big tarpon, as well as crabs, oysters, and shrimp.

The state of Mississippi protects a number of its endangered animals. Black bears, Florida panthers, gray bats, Indiana bats, sea turtles, gopher tortoises, sawback turtles (black-knobbed, ringed, and yellow-blotched), black pine snakes, eastern indigo snakes, rainbow snakes, and southern hognose snakes are on the endangered animals list in Mississippi.

About 100 years ago, wood ducks were nearly extinct. Today, their numbers have increased greatly.

Mississippi has a mix of both undeveloped areas and urban areas, such as the city of Jackson, seen here.

Plants & Animals

Pitcher Plant

Pitcher plants grow in the damp bogs of Mississippi. They resemble pitchers because they hold water. These plants also devour insects. The plant's sweet nectar attracts insects into its tube-shaped leaves. Once inside, the insects become trapped in the hairs that cover the leaf's interior. Enzymes, which are juices at the bottom of the leafy tube, break down the insects so that the plant can digest them and use them as food.

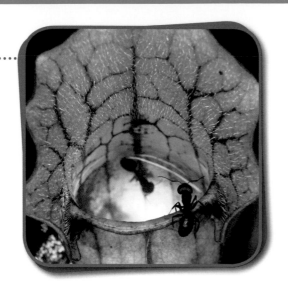

Bald Cypress

Long ago, ancient forests of bald cypresses grew in swamp water or near the Mississippi River. Bald cypresses can still be seen in Mississippi, but many of these majestic trees have been cut down for their valuable timber. The tall, old trees have knobby roots and branches of needles, rather than leaves.

Sandhill Crane

Mississippi's sandhill cranes are an endangered species. Standing about 4 feet (1.2 m) tall, with a nearly 6-foot-(1.8 m) wingspan, they have long legs and necks. Their feathers are shades of gray. Sandhill cranes have a red crown, white cheek patches, and black legs. The call of a sandhill crane is a loud, distinctive, croaking sound.

American Alligator

For a time, American alligators were an endangered species. Today, though, their numbers are growing. In 2005, the American alligator was declared Mississippi's state reptile. Male alligators grow up to 15 feet (4.6 m) long, and the average gator has 75 teeth.

Wild Turkey

In the early 1900s, wild turkeys were nearly hunted to extinction. Because of the efforts of Mississippi's wildlife experts, however, today the state has one of the largest wild turkey populations in the country, with about 250,000 birds.

Black Bear

Mississippi's hardwood bottomlands once supported large populations of black bears. These small bears nearly died out in the twentieth century due to excessive hunting and the disappearance of hardwood forests due to lumbering and farming. In 2002 wildlife experts estimated there were fewer than 50 bears in the state. Today, they believe that number has more than doubled!

From the Beginning

Thousands of years ago, humans came to live on the land that would one day become Mississippi. The land was an ideal place for these hunting and gathering people to settle down. Its many rivers provided water to drink, fish to eat, and an easy way to travel and trade goods. The forests were full of animals to hunt for food and wood to use for building simple shelters and dugout canoes. These early people soon discovered that they did not always have to hunt animals and gather fruit and nuts for all their food. They could settle down and grow some of the food they needed in the area's rich soil.

The Mississippi River gave these early groups so much that many of them considered it to be the center of the universe. Archaeologists, the scientists who study the past, have found evidence that these early people built small cities and farming communities in several areas of the land that is now Mississippi. The archaeologists have unearthed stone and metal tools, weapons, pottery, masks, and engraved seashells that indicate busy, successful communities. These experts believe that the ancient people they call Mound Builders built the huge mounds of earth located around Mississippi and other nearby states. These early people probably honored their leaders and their dead by building homes and temples on the flat tops of some of these mounds.

Some families left Mississippi to look for work during the Great Depression of the 1930s.

The Native Groups

Experts believe that over time the descendents of the Mound Builders organized themselves into separate villages and groups. These communities survived by hunting, fishing, and farming. The people used dugout canoes to travel and trade along the coastal shores and on the rivers. They probably lived in shelters made of leaves and wooden poles or log houses plastered with clay from nearby riverbanks. Living in separate areas, these individual communities eventually developed their own languages and customs.

One such group was the Chickasaw. Some experts believe the Chickasaw and the Choctaw may have been part of one group in earlier times. Spread across Mississippi, Alabama, Tennessee, and Kentucky, the Chickasaw were

This mound is located in Illinois. The people who built it were from the Mississippian culture, which first developed in the Mississippi River Valley and flourished in many areas of North America before the arrival of European explorers.

The Natchez people used natural grasses and clay to build dwellings similar to this one shown at Grand Village of the Natchez, a reconstructed community in Natchez, Mississippi.

This painting from the mid-1800s shows Choctaw Indians playing a ball game similar to modern lacrosse.

seminomadic. They moved part of the time and settled along waterways within their territory at other times. Members of their group hunted, gathered, and grew enough food to feed their own people. Chickasaw society was well organized, with strong leaders and good lines of communication. Runners carried messages along the Chickasaw network to far-scattered people whenever they needed to hold a meeting, or council. Chickasaw defenses were so strong that they boasted their members were almost never captured or killed.

To the south and east into Alabama lived the Choctaw, a forest people who also farmed and traded. Like the other groups in the area, the Choctaw were well organized. Their central government included courts where elders could listen to group members' complaints and settle them. Many Choctaw males had sloping flat foreheads. Ethnologists (the historians who study ancient people) believed members of the group pressed boards against boy babies' foreheads to give them their distinctive shape. This made them identifiable as Choctaw and set them apart from the men of other native groups. Early European explorers noted

MAKING A SHELL GORGET

Shell gorgets (pronounced GOR-jetz) were carved-shell ornaments found in some Mississippi Valley burial sites, dating from about AD 1000 to 1600. Images on the gorgets included rattlesnakes, falcons, a "birdman" with human and bird features, and many other natural images. Follow these instructions to make your own gorgets.

WHAT YOU NEED

- large, clean shells of any kind (you can collect them from outside or buy some at craft supply shops)
- pencil
- thin-point markers
- 3-foot-long (.9 m) lengths of cord or ribbon
- strong glue

DESIGNING A SHELL GORGET:

Decide on an animal, bird, reptile, or other image from nature for your shell gorget. In pencil, sketch your design inside the shell. Once you are happy with the design, trace over your pencil markings with a marker. Tie the ends of the cord or ribbon into a small tight knot. Rest this knot on the back of your shell. Use the strong glue to make the ribbon stick to the shell. When the glue is dry you might also want to use strong tape to make sure the shell sticks to the ribbon. Wear the gorget, give it as a gift, or hang it to display it to your friends and family!

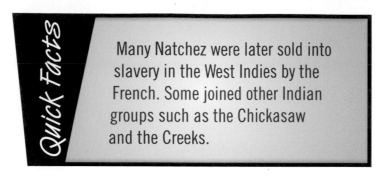
that the Choctaw were fast runners who also loved to play ball games. Players sometimes peacefully settled disputes with other groups by playing stickball.

The Natchez people lived along the Mississippi River. At least five hundred years ago, they used the river's waters and rich bottomlands to grow corn, squash, and beans. They organized their society into separate classes of nobility (rulers) and commoners (ordinary people). The Natchez had one supreme ruler, called the Great Sun, who was so honored that he was carried everywhere so he never had to touch the ground.

This illustration shows a scene from the 1801 novella *Atala*, by François-René de Chateaubriand. The story is about a Natchez Indian named Chactas, seen on the left.

This painting by William Powell portrays Spanish explorer Hernando de Soto's discovery of the Mississippi River in 1541. Historians believe de Soto died on the banks of the river one year later.

Many of the place names in Mississippi, such as Biloxi, Yazoo, and Pascagoula, come from Native American languages. According to Muriel H. Wright, a historian who wrote a book about the history of the Mississippi River, the Chippewa word "Mississippi" has been translated as "great river" or "gathering of waters." According to Choctaw legend, when their ancestors came upon the river, they exclaimed, "Misha sipokni!" That phrase has been translated as "Here is a river that is beyond all age!"

Natives and Europeans Meet

The Spanish explorer Hernando de Soto and an army of several hundred soldiers became the first Europeans ever to see what is now the state of Mississippi. Searching for treasure in 1540, the members of this expedition began their explorations in Florida and ended beyond the Rio Grande River in the Southwest. When de Soto's group passed through the area that is present-day Mississippi, it encountered members of three Native American nations: the Natchez, the Choctaw, and the Chickasaw. The Chickasaw were the people with whom de Soto had the most contact. The Chickasaw did not welcome the contact, though. They attacked de Soto's party several times until the Spaniards left the area.

Louis XIV ruled France from 1643 to 1715.

In 1673, 130 years after de Soto's visit to America, the French explorers Jacques Marquette and Louis Jolliet came down the Mississippi River. They turned around when they reached a village at the mouth of the Arkansas River, populated by Native Americans called the Arkansas. The two explorers did not travel any farther because they feared meeting enemy Spaniards, who were also exploring the area.

In 1682 a French explorer called Sieur de La Salle also traveled down the Mississippi River to the Gulf of Mexico. La Salle recorded meeting people of the Taensa, Natchez, and Choctaw groups. When La Salle reached the mouth of the Mississippi, he claimed all the land along the huge river on behalf of his ruler, King Louis XIV of France.

In the years that followed, the French made several efforts to create colonies on the land La Salle had claimed. They wanted to prevent their Spanish rivals to the south from gaining complete control of the land that would eventually become the southern part of the United States. In 1699, Pierre Le Moyne d'Iberville brought two hundred settlers to a location in what is the present-day Bay of Biloxi. The group built Fort Maurepas. According to Iberville's plans, this would become the first capital of French Louisiana.

Eventually the French built several plantations around Fort Maurepas. In 1719, the plantation owners imported slaves from Africa and forced these slaves to work without pay in the cotton, tobacco, rice, and indigo fields.

In the meantime, the British had also started colonies in North America. That led to conflicts with the French. Soon the British and French engaged in what would be called the French and Indian War, which lasted from 1754 to 1763. The name of the French and Indian War refers to fighting that occurred between the French, who were supported by their Native American allies, and the British, who had their own Native American allies in the fight. After the British defeated the French, Great Britain gained all of France's territories east of the Mississippi River, with the exception of the city of New Orleans. British government officials in London made southern Mississippi part of the British colony of West Florida. Northern Mississippi became part of Britain's Georgia colony.

Meanwhile, trouble was brewing in the British colonies. In 1775, many colonists became frustrated with the British rulers and began the American Revolution. However, the people who lived in what is now Mississippi did not become involved in the fighting of that war. Most residents of West Florida

The French and Indian War was part of a larger conflict called the Seven Years' War, which involved many countries around the world.

were Loyalists, or Tories, who remained loyal to Britain's King George III. They hoped the British redcoats would win the war. In 1781, the war directly affected the people of West Florida. Spain took control of West Florida while the British were fighting the French. When the Revolution came to an end two years later, the colonies separated from Great Britain and became the United States. Great Britain formally recognized Spain as West Florida's owner. Spain granted some northern land to the newly formed United States. In 1795, a new treaty stated that West Florida's northern boundary was changed. This meant that most of present-day Mississippi became part of the United States.

The Mississippi Territory

In 1798, the US federal government organized this newly acquired land into the Mississippi Territory. Roughly twice the size of the state today, this territory reached from the Chattahoochee River on the east to the Mississippi River on the west. The territory included most of the present-day states of Alabama and Mississippi.

In 1803, the United States expanded when President Thomas Jefferson completed the Louisiana Purchase. That added close to 3 million square miles (7,769,966 sq km) of western land to the United States, including the city of New Orleans. Americans became more involved in trade up and down the Mississippi River. One year later, the United States government extended the territory's boundary farther north than it had been. The territory now included everything up to the southern border of Tennessee.

In 1810, British settlers in West Florida rejected Spanish rule and declared themselves the independent Republic of West Florida. However, President James Madison had other ideas. He made the republic part of the United States. Two years later, West Florida was formally attached to the eastern part of the territory of Mississippi.

Statehood

By 1817, the population of the Mississippi Territory had grown so much, the federal government divided it in two. The western half was admitted into the Union as the state of Mississippi. The eastern half became the Alabama Territory, which would become a state in 1819.

To do the backbreaking work of growing cotton in ever-larger fields, plantation owners continued to buy more and more slaves. Cotton had soon made Mississippi one of the richest states in the Union. Several wealthy white families lived in huge plantation homes or in elegant mansions in the busy, cultured city of Natchez. However, Mississippi had many more white families who farmed small pieces of land or ran small businesses.

Mississippi's large black population included a few hundred free blacks who lived and worked in the state. The slave population, however, numbered in the tens of thousands. Natchez had the second largest slave market in the United

Profits from slave labor helped build elegant plantations, such as Stanton Hall in Natchez, Mississippi. Many plantations can be visited today.

States, where about 200,000 slaves were bought and sold.

The lives of slaves were largely ones of endless work. Owners sometimes split up slave families and sold the children to other plantations. Slaves often lived in broken-down cabins. They lacked basic necessities, such as enough food and clothing.

The Civil War

By the middle of the 1800s, Americans were involved in a heated argument about whether the practice of slavery should expand in the United States. Many people in the South wanted slavery to continue and grow. Their economy depended on it. They realized their region could not prosper as it had without the free labor of slaves. Many people in the North, on the other hand, wanted to ban the import, sale, and use of slaves. This argument over slavery and another fight over states' rights caused the Civil War, which began in 1861. That is when Southern states voted to secede, or withdraw, from the Union. South Carolina was the first to do so. On January 9, 1861, Mississippi became the second state to secede. The Southern states then formed their own new nation, which they called the Confederate States of America.

The Civil War was a devastating period for Mississippi. The Union and Confederate armies fought many important battles in the state. A ferocious battle took place at Vicksburg when Union soldiers occupied the city during a forty-seven-day siege. The Union soldiers took over the port and destroyed businesses, churches, and homes. Confederate soldiers fought hard to defend Vicksburg during the siege. Without incoming food, supplies, and reinforcements, though, Confederate soldiers in Vicksburg finally surrendered.

Of the 78,000 Mississippi men and boys who fought for the Confederate army, approximately 12,000 died in battle and 15,000 died of disease. The rest had been weakened by their lack of food, warm clothing, and shoes. The women, children, and old people who remained at home also suffered terribly. Many women took on the kind of hard, physical work formerly done by men. Like the soldiers, the women endured hunger, poverty, and sickness.

Mississippi's black population suffered during the Civil War as well. However, their future seemed brighter when President Abraham Lincoln declared all slaves to be free. While Lincoln's Emancipation Proclamation did free the slaves, life was still hard. There were few jobs to be had during or after the war for people of color. Like many white families, black families found it difficult to feed, house, and clothe themselves.

After the Civil War

Hard times continued in Mississippi in the years after the Civil War. The US government declared that the Southern states could reenter the Union, but first these states had to undergo reconstruction. The US government used its army to

Some Vicksburg residents hid in forests and caves outside their city in order to escape the deadly fighting in 1863.

run the Southern states. It placed all of them, including Mississippi, under military law. The federal government told the Southern states when elections would be held and dictated who could run for office.

During the Reconstruction Era (1865-1877), Mississippi drew up a new state constitution. The constitution gave African Americans the right to vote and to hold political office. It also made all children eligible for free public education. Although black Mississippians enjoyed newfound freedoms for a time, those liberties did not last. After Mississippi was formally readmitted to the Union, white politicians worked to regain the political power they had lost. They passed a new constitution that denied the state's black population many basic rights, such as the right to vote and the right to own property.

Change Comes Slowly

Mississippi's economy remained devastated for many decades after the Civil War. Without slave labor, the state never became rich from cotton again. After many big plantations fell into ruin, small farmers struggled to grow crops they could sell for a decent profit. These small farmers, called sharecroppers, leased land from large landowners to whom they had to pay part of every crop. This tenant farm system made it hard for sharecroppers to get ahead financially, though. For decades, Mississippi remained one of the poorest states in the United States.

More hard times were on the way. In 1927, a devastating flood caused tens of thousands of Mississippians to leave their homes. When the country entered the Great Depression in 1929, Mississippians suffered even more. Many of them found it so hard to earn a living that they fled Mississippi. They headed north, hoping to find work in factories in cities such as New York City, Philadelphia, and Chicago. Times were tough across the country, though. Many businesses closed and many people lost their jobs. The government established programs to help the unemployed. The economy also improved when the country entered World War II. Jobs were created as supplies were needed for the war effort.

During this time, many blacks left Mississippi to escape racism. State laws kept segregation in place in Mississippi until well into the 1960s. Segregation laws stated that black people could not use the same facilities as whites. African Americans could not eat in certain restaurants or attend the same schools. In addition, African Americans continued to be denied the right to vote.

Beginning in the late 1950s, individuals began to fight this unfair system and the civil rights movement got underway. In the 1960s, tensions grew in Mississippi between people who wanted to work for equality and those who wanted to keep segregation laws. Race riots broke out after a young man named

Both black and white sharecroppers throughout the South struggled to make a living on farms.

The 1966 March Against Fear at the Mississippi State Capitol marked a turning point in the struggle for civil rights for all people.

James Meredith tried to become the first black student to enroll at the University of Mississippi. When President John F. Kennedy sent federal troops to try to stop the riots, the troops came under attack.

In 1965, the passage of the Voting Rights Act by Congress meant that Mississippi state officials could no longer deny African Americans the chance to vote. From that point on, Mississippi's black population steadily gained political power. In 1969, the Supreme Court ruled in favor of desegregation. That meant both black and white children had to attend the same schools. Desegregation did not go well at first. Many white parents removed their children from public schools and sent them to private schools instead. At the same time, the number of black school principals and teachers actually declined, as parents pressured schools to hire whites only. However, many educational reforms took place in the 1980s, and the quality of public education in Mississippi improved.

Mississippi's economy also grew in the 1980s and the 1990s. Agriculture became more varied and no longer depended so heavily on cotton. The state also began to promote tourism and invited visitors to enjoy its wild natural areas and historic sites. Tourism created many new jobs in hotels, restaurants, parks, historic sites, and riverboat casinos.

Important Dates

★ **1540** Spaniard Hernando de Soto leads the first group of Europeans across what is present-day Mississippi on a search for treasure through the South.

★ **1673** French explorers Jacques Marquette and Louis Jolliet begin exploration of the Mississippi River.

★ **1682** Sieur de La Salle travels the Mississippi River, claiming all lands drained by the river for the king of France.

★ **1699** The French build Fort Maurepas, the first French settlement in what will become Mississippi, near Biloxi.

★ **1763** The area that is present-day Mississippi passes into English control at the end of the French and Indian War.

★ **1798** The western part of land that will become the state of Mississippi is organized as an American territory.

★ **1803** The Louisiana Purchase opens the Mississippi River to American trade.

★ **1812** The War of 1812 begins.

★ **1817** Mississippi is admitted to the Union as the 20th state.

★ **1861** On January 9, Mississippi becomes the second Southern state to secede from the Union. The Civil War begins.

★ **1939** Oil is discovered near Tinsley, in Yazoo County.

★ **1964** Congress passes the Civil Rights Act, outlawing segregation in public places. Fannie Lou Hamer helps to organize Freedom Summer, an effort to register African-American voters in Mississippi.

★ **1986** The Tennessee-Tombigbee Waterway is completed.

★ **2005** Hurricane Katrina comes ashore, affecting the states of Mississippi, Louisiana, Alabama, Florida, and parts of Texas. It causes billions of dollars in damage and kills more than a thousand people.

★ **2011** Record-setting floods destroy hundreds of homes along the Mississippi River.

The People

Five hundred years ago, only Native Americans lived in the region that would later become Mississippi. Even after European explorers reported that the land had the possibility of becoming a bountiful place to live, few white settlers came. When some French settlers arrived in 1699, they settled near present-day Biloxi. The area seemed to offer a natural port for shipping, rich soil for farming, and fresh drinking water in its rivers.

By the early 1700s, Native Americans shared the land with just a few French neighbors. The second French settlement in the area was founded in 1716. Everything changed with the arrival of slaves whom the French had brought to the area from Africa. Slaves who could work the land without pay changed the area's fortunes and population. With free labor, the land could be farmed for great profit. This possibility attracted the interest of Great Britain, Spain, and France. Great Britain already had settlers in the northeast and Spain had settlers in the southwest. Soon Great Britain and France were fighting over land claims. France finally gave up its land claims to Great Britain after losing the French and Indian War in 1760.

In Their Own Words

That Mississippi sound, that Delta sound, is in them old records. You can hear it all the way through.

—Muddy Waters, blues musician

Mississippians enjoy many fairs and festivals throughout the year.

A Choctaw boy dances at a festival on a reservation in Philadelphia, Mississippi.

Population of Mississippi in 2010

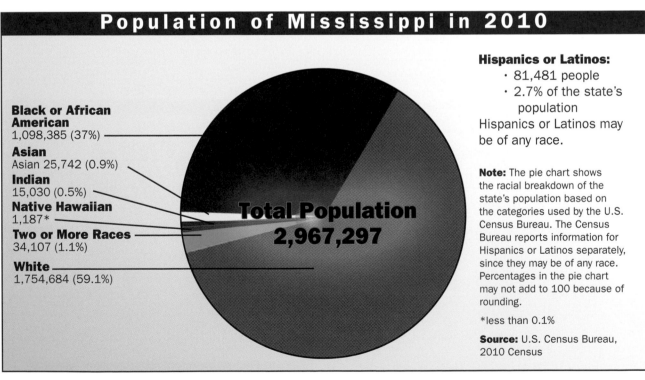

Black or African American
1,098,385 (37%)

Asian
Asian 25,742 (0.9%)

Indian
15,030 (0.5%)

Native Hawaiian
1,187*

Two or More Races
34,107 (1.1%)

White
1,754,684 (59.1%)

Total Population
2,967,297

Hispanics or Latinos:
· 81,481 people
· 2.7% of the state's population
Hispanics or Latinos may be of any race.

Note: The pie chart shows the racial breakdown of the state's population based on the categories used by the U.S. Census Bureau. The Census Bureau reports information for Hispanics or Latinos separately, since they may be of any race. Percentages in the pie chart may not add to 100 because of rounding.

*less than 0.1%

Source: U.S. Census Bureau, 2010 Census

The first Spaniards who passed through what is now Mississippi came and left the area quickly. Today's Hispanic families are among the fastest-growing groups of residents in the state.

During the short period between that war and the outbreak of the American Revolution, most of the settlers who arrived in the area were British. They came from England, Ireland, Scotland, and Wales. Spain also sent settlers to America. During the Revolution, Spain took the opportunity to seize control of West Florida, which contained part of present-day Mississippi.

After the United States gained its independence from Great Britain in 1783, the population grew quickly. Native Americans, white settlers from Europe, and slaves from Africa made up the population. Newcomers kept arriving in great numbers.

By 1800, about 7,000 Native Americans still lived in what is now Mississippi. In the Natchez area alone, the population numbered between 4,000 and 5,000 whites and blacks, which made it quite a sizeable city for its time. Approximately 1,200 white settlers and slaves lived along the Tombigbee River.

Increasing numbers of white settlers pushed Native Americans from the territories where they had lived for thousands of years. In 1816, one traveler reported that 4,000 settlers came to the Mississippi River area in just nine days. Between 1810 and 1820, the population soared from approximately 37,000 people to about 75,000 people, including slaves. By 1860, the population had grown to nearly 800,000 people. On the eve of the Civil War, Mississippi's population was about evenly divided between black and white people.

Growth slowed significantly after the end of slavery weakened the economy. New settlers found other parts of the United States more attractive than the southern United States. By 1900, Mississippi had just over 1.5 million people. Between 1910 and 1920, the population actually decreased by several thousand. Mississippi's population went through a series of small increases followed by small decreases over the next few decades. In 2012, about 2,984,926 people lived in the state. And while the population is growing, it has remained relatively small compared to other states. For example, the state of Mississippi's population is just slightly higher than that of the city of Chicago.

African Americans made up the majority of Mississippi's population until 1940. Today, however, about 60 percent of Mississippi's population is white. African Americans make up approximately 37 percent of Mississippians. The state has the highest percentage of black people of any state.

In 2012, around 26,000 Asians and Asian Americans lived in Mississippi. This includes many Filipinos (people from the Philippines) and Vietnamese people who have recently moved to the state. Many came to work in Mississippi's fishing and shrimping industries, while others worked in other Mississippi industries.

The number of Hispanics is increasing rapidly in Mississippi. In 2010 there were more than 81,000 Hispanic residents. Many of them are Mexican Americans or Mexicans who have come to the state to work in agriculture. Hispanic populations are growing in Mississippi's cities as well.

In a state with so many agricultural resources, most Mississippians have long chosen to live in rural farming areas. Mississippi's cities have remained small. The largest city, Jackson, has a population of approximately 174,000 people. Biloxi, another major city, is just a quarter the size of Jackson. Hattiesburg, Meridian, and Gulfport also have populations of slightly more than 40,000. Fewer than 400,000 of the state's residents live in a sizeable city.

Small town storefronts in some parts of Mississippi look much the way they did 100 years ago.

Diverse Influences

Today, as in the past, people of diverse origins call Mississippi home. Many of the state's residents have lived in the state all their lives, but Mississippi's population also includes many people who have only recently arrived. Some of these are immigrants, or people who have come from another country to live and to work in the United States. Others have moved to Mississippi from elsewhere in the United States. Some families come because of job opportunities. Many people who move to Mississippi are retirees. They come to spend their later years enjoying the state's restful environment, mild climate, and beautiful scenery.

Cultural influences from a variety of ethnicities can be seen in the state of Mississippi. Native American culture is still visible. Tourists visit the state to see evidence of the great Mound Builder civilization that developed here a thousand years ago. Although the Mound Builders are long gone, their descendents in other Native American groups remain in Mississippi.

Some descendants of the Chickasaw, the Choctaw, and the Natchez who were living there when the French arrived in the seventeenth century continue to live in Mississippi. The current Natchez Native American population is small

Famous Mississippians

Oprah Winfrey: Television Star

Oprah Winfrey was born in Kosciusko in 1954. Raised in a rural area in a poor family, Oprah studied hard and began working at a radio station while still in high school. Today, she is one of the richest people in the United States and beloved by her fans. She runs her own production company and television network and has written books, published magazines, and has donated money to many charities.

William Faulkner: Author

Winner of the 1949 Nobel Prize in Literature, William Faulkner was not only born and raised in Mississippi, he also used the state as the setting in many of his books. He grew up in Oxford, but in his novels, Faulkner renamed the town Jefferson. Faulkner died in 1962.

Jim Henson: Muppet Creator

Jim Henson was born in 1936 in Greenville, Mississippi, and was raised in Leland. He created the *Sesame Street* Muppets, including Kermit, Miss Piggy, Big Bird, Cookie Monster, Bert and Ernie, and Gonzo. Henson died in 1990. The town of Leland has opened a Jim Henson museum honoring his work.

B. B. King: Blues Musician

B. B. King, one of the world's great blues musicians, was born in Itta Bena in 1925. He was the child of a sharecropper, and as a little boy went out into the fields to pick cotton. He first played the guitar as a child. By the 1940s, he was performing on the radio. In the 1950s, he had a long string of hit songs. Today a new generation loves to listen to him play his guitar, which he has named Lucille.

Elvis Presley: Rock and Roll Musician

Elvis Presley, called the King of Rock and Roll, was born in Tupelo in 1935. One of the greatest musicians of all time, Elvis had 149 songs on *Billboard Magazine*'s "Hot 100 Pop Chart." Eighteen of them occupied the top spot on the charts. That achievement has never been matched by another singer. Visitors still flock to Tupelo to see the tiny house that was his birthplace. Elvis died in 1977.

Medgar Evers: Civil Rights Activist

Medgar Evers was born in Decatur in 1925. After earning his bachelors degree from Alcorn College, he applied to the University of Mississippi Law School in 1954. His rejection from the school highlighted the school's segregation policies and Evers became a leader in the civil rights movement. In 1963, Evers was assassinated by a white supremacist. However, Evers's legacy has lived on and inspired many.

and scattered throughout the state, as is the Chickasaw. Nevertheless, museums and cultural centers celebrate their heritage. Mississippi has always had a larger number of Choctaw. Today thousands live on the Choctaw Reservation, located on Highway 16, in the middle of the state near the town of Philadelphia.

Despite the early Spanish explorations, little of that early Spanish influence remains visible today. The French, who followed the Spaniards into the area, left their mark in a few place names, such as Bienville and Bay St. Louis. Louisville was named after France's King Louis XIV. As recently as 100 years ago, though, so many people of French descent still lived in the state that French classes were taught in most Mississippi schools. According to one historian, "many people born in the early twentieth century can recall relatives who spoke only or mainly French."

One can also see a few signs of Asian influence in Mississippi. The Chinese, who came to work on cotton plantations in the nineteenth century after the slaves were freed, formed a tightly knit group. One group, from China's Sze Yap district, first lived in Washington County. Later on, another group owned land in Boliver County. A few Chinese grocery stores can be found around Mississippi. The town of Greenville has a separate Chinese cemetery. Today you can also see store signs written in Vietnamese in Biloxi and other places along the coast where Vietnamese people work as shrimpers. One of the most significant changes in Mississippi's population in recent years has been in the number of Asian Americans living there.

Throughout Mississippi's history, African Americans have had a big influence on life in the state. Many own farms and businesses. Some are active in politics. Particularly in the Delta Region, African-American musicians created a unique kind of music called the blues. Some of this music has a haunting, mournful sound, while some blues songs are lively and fast. Once a branch of folk music, the blues have greatly influenced other types of music, especially rock and roll.

Mississippi for Visitors

Mississippians cherish their heritage. They have preserved many of the state's elegant old homes and neighborhoods. Historical sites also include reminders of difficult times in Mississippi's history, particularly its years of slavery and the Civil War. A historical marker at the site of Natchez's Forks of the Road notes the location of a slave market. Civil War buffs can visit many of Mississippi's battle sites, some of which have been turned into parks or posted with historical markers. Some Civil War groups stage reenactments of famous battles.

Many Mississippians also enjoy sports and the outdoors. Along with out-of-state tourists, they flock to the state's parks, waterways, and other natural areas. Many Mississippians like to hunt, fish, and hike. The state boasts more than fifty state wildlife management areas, fourteen national wildlife refuges, and

Musicians of many races and musical styles have embraced the blues that African Americans developed in the Mississippi Delta.

Reminders of the Civil War are never far away in Mississippi.

six national forests. Visitors to the Panther Swamp National Wildlife Refuge, for example, can observe American alligators, otters, swamp rabbits, and mink living in the wild. Visitors to the Gulf Islands National Seashore can sunbathe, swim, or enjoy boating along the white beaches and sparkling ocean. Coastal marshes are popular places for hikers. Mississippi's many rivers, lakes, bayous, and oceans are paradises for the state's fishermen and women.

Many residents of Mississippi are avid sports fans. Residents closely follow state universities' teams, including the University of Mississippi, or Ole Miss, Rebels and the Mississippi State Bulldogs.

Eating in this top agricultural and fishing state is a delicious experience for Mississippians and tourists alike. The town of Belzoni is often called the farm-raised catfish capital of the world. About 60 percent of the farm-raised catfish in the US are grown near Belzoni. Fried catfish is a favorite dish throughout the state. Mississippi is famous for its dark rich soil and for its Mississippi mud pies. This thick, gooey chocolate pie resembles the state's thick, dark mud seen in swamps, riverbanks, and bottomlands. Visitors can find sweet potato dishes on restaurant menus throughout the state, which is a major sweet potato grower.

Birdwatchers spot plenty of birds near Mississippi's many waterways.

Sweet potato pie is a special favorite at Thanksgiving around the country, but especially in Mississippi. The Mississippi shrimp boils are a delicious feature of many outdoor festivals. Shrimp boils are big pots of shrimp along with meats, vegetables, and spices.

Art and music lovers can find museums, galleries, and concert halls all over the state. The fine art museums include the Ohr-O'Keefe Museum of Art, in Biloxi, the Walter Anderson Museum of Art, in Ocean Springs, the Lauren Rogers Museum of Art, in Laurel, and the Mississippi Museum of Art, in Jackson.

Classical music lovers attend concerts in Jackson, which has its own symphony, and at colleges and universities around the state. Mississippians listen to great music, not just in concert halls, but in churches, at county fairs, and at family reunions.

Mississippi's many festivals attract families from all around the region to celebrate the state's rich land, history, great food, wonderful music, and colorful art. The town of Tupelo, for example, throws an Elvis Presley festival once a year.

Calendar of Events

★ **Dixie National Livestock Show and Rodeo**

The city of Jackson hosts this celebration every January through early February. The event includes a parade, a rodeo, several livestock shows (including one where kids show off the farm animals they have raised), a dance, and more.

★ **Carnival on the Coast**

These Mardi Gras celebrations are held on the Gulf Coast and in Natchez every year at the beginning of Lent, which falls in February or March. People celebrate Mardi Gras by dressing up in outrageous costumes and going to more than twenty parades.

★ **Annual World Catfish Festival**

Mississippi's catfish are honored each April in Belzoni. The town hosts a fishing competition, a catfish-eating contest, and even a Miss Catfish pageant!

★ Blessing of the Fleet and Seafood Festival

A special ceremony every May and June honors fishermen and shrimp harvesters who died at sea. A wreath is dropped into the water at the Biloxi Yacht Club pier. A bishop blesses the boats as they participate in a procession. The Biloxi Seafood Festival in September is another seaside celebration. Events include a schooner boat race and shrimp-eating feasts.

★ Ocean Springs Art Walk

This art fair features more than seventy local artists. There are gallery tours, music, food, and art activities for kids.

★ Choctaw Indian Fair

The Choctaw community invites everyone to come to its fair, held every July, on their reservation in Mississippi. Visitors flock to the event to experience traditional Native American dances, music, and arts and crafts.

★ Mississippi Delta Blues and Heritage Festival

In Greenville, music is in the air every September thanks to its many concerts. Musicians celebrate Mississippi's Delta blues tradition with nonstop music during the festival.

★ Mississippi State Fair

In this rich farming state, the fall harvest is celebrated in Jackson every October. One of the South's largest state fairs, the fair gives farmers a chance to show off their finest stock animals and produce. There are also carnival rides and plenty to eat.

★ Sweet Potato Festival

Vardaman, which calls itself the "Sweet Potato Capital of the World," honors its favorite crop every November. Visitors sample all kinds of sweet potatoes and can purchase a cookbook full of sweet potato recipes.

How the Government Works

Mississippi, like other states, has several levels of government that serve its people at different levels, including federal, state, county, city, and town.

On the federal level, citizens of every state, including Mississippi, elect two US senators every six years. The number of representatives a state has in the US House of Representatives varies according to the size of the state's population. Mississippi has four representatives. Both senators and representatives work on behalf of all Americans. They also pay special attention to the needs and concerns of the people of their own state. Mississippians also participate in US presidential elections, which are held every four years.

The Political History of Mississippi

Mississippi became a state in 1817. When it formally entered the Union as a state, Mississippi needed a state constitution. Political leaders wrote one immediately. Three other versions followed in 1832, 1869, and 1890.

The Mississippi State Capitol in Jackson

Haley Barbour, born in Yazoo City, served as Mississippi's governor from 2004 to 2012.

The state constitution spells out how the state's government works. Mississippi's constitution, in its current form, provides for a governor and lieutenant governor to be elected every four years. These officials can serve only two terms in their lifetime. The governor is the highest office in the state. He or she is responsible for seeing that the laws of the state are upheld. He or she can also convene, or bring together, the state legislature and grant pardons. The constitution also spells out which other officers are to be elected, rather than appointed. As in other states, Mississippi also has a two-chamber legislature and a court system.

Like other voters in the United States, many Mississippians belong to one of the two major political parties: the Democrats or the Republicans. As in most of the country, the majority of Mississippi's local, state, and national representatives belong to one of those two political groups.

For most of Mississippi's history, the right to vote was restricted to certain people. Women did not win voting rights until the 1920s. In a new state constitution in 1890, Mississippi curbed African Americans' right to vote, though they had been able to vote during the Reconstruction Era. In protests and marches, African Americans, along with many whites, pressured the federal government to pass the Voting Rights Act of 1965. This law gave African Americans the right to vote again in their states.

Marchers protesting the murders of three civil rights workers in 1964 demonstrated their outrage in a procession to Philadelphia, Mississippi.

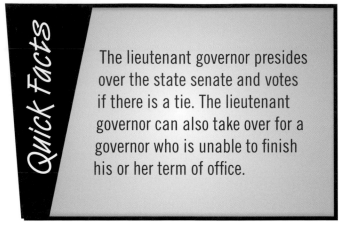

The lieutenant governor presides over the state senate and votes if there is a tie. The lieutenant governor can also take over for a governor who is unable to finish his or her term of office.

How a Bill Becomes a State Law

The power to make and pass laws in Mississippi involves the governor as well as state legislators elected to one of two "houses." These houses are the state senate and the house of representatives. A senator or a house representative may introduce a bill (a proposed law) of interest to citizens. The senator or representative reads the bill in his or her house. Leaders of that house assign the bill to a committee that specializes in the issue, such as education, transportation, or the environment. The committee studies the bill. When it decides the entire senate or house should hear the bill, the committee schedules a date to do so. After the bill is read, it is put to a vote. If the bill passes in the house where it was read, it is sent to the other house, where the bill goes through the same process.

Bills may be sent back and forth depending on changes that representatives make along the way. Sometimes a bill goes straight to the governor, who signs it into law. However, sometimes the governor vetoes, or refuses to sign the bill. When that happens, the bill may go back to the senate or house of representatives for more changes. The governor may then sign it. However, if the governor still vetoes the bill, the legislators can still get it passed. They can override the governor's veto if they have enough votes to pass the bill.

A bill may also go back to the legislature for changes before it ever gets to the governor. At each step, the legislators, including the special committees, must review the changes in the bill before it goes to the governor. The result is called a compromise bill, or one that must satisfy both houses.

Branches of Government

The state government in Mississippi is divided into three branches, as in other states.

EXECUTIVE ★ ★ ★ ★ ★ ★ ★ ★
The executive branch is charged with preparing budgets and making sure the laws passed by the legislative branch are carried out. This branch includes the governor, lieutenant governor, and other officials such as the secretary of state, treasurer, auditor, and the attorney general.

LEGISLATIVE ★ ★ ★ ★ ★ ★ ★ ★
The legislative branch is made up of the state senate, with 52 members, and the house of representatives, which has 122 members. Its job is to make and pass state laws.

JUDICIAL ★ ★ ★ ★ ★ ★ ★ ★
At the top of the judicial branch sits the Mississippi supreme court, the court of appeals, and trial courts. Lower courts include circuit courts, chancery courts, county courts, justice courts, and municipal or town courts. All the courts rule on matters of state law.

In the 1960s, the federal government sent representatives to help unregistered Mississippi residents vote for the first time.

The Mississippi Band of Choctaw Indians has its own government. Recognized by the US government since 1945, the Choctaw people have their own constitution. It spells out the organization of a Choctaw government council that represents all its members.

How the State's Local Government Works

Mississippi is divided into eighty-two counties. Unlike the systems in many other states, an elected five-member board of supervisors runs each county. County boards of supervisors set property taxes. They may decide such matters as which county roads big trucks may travel on, for example. The state also has a total of more than 290 cities and towns with their own local governments. The mayors of most of these cities and towns work with an elected council to make decisions concerning local laws and their enforcement. Mayors and councils pass laws that affect the people who live in their town. They might decide, for instance, where new factories can be built. Such matters are covered by what are called zoning laws.

Hot Topics

Just as in other states, political issues come and go in Mississippi. After Hurricane Katrina, residents of the state were concerned about how much help the federal government would be able to provide to rebuild.

Every day, Mississippians participate in their government and voice their opinions. They write, e-mail, and call their legislators to talk about the issues that concern them. Legislation is often shaped by the voice of the people. By learning about issues, everyone can make a difference.

In 1993 a lawsuit was filed in the Mississippi court system against the governor of the state. The people who filed the lawsuit wanted the state to stop flying the state flag that included part of a Confederate battle flag. A state commission recommended that a new flag be designed and voted on by Mississippians. A majority of the people voted to keep the flag as it was. Today, many people still sign petitions to get the state to change the flag.

This kind of public activism keeps Mississippians involved in their government. Mississippians decide their future by their votes and by reminding the people they elect to listen to their voices.

Contacting Lawmakers

★ ★ ★ ★ ★ ★ ★ ★ ★ ★ ★ ★

If you are interested in contacting Mississippi's state legislators, go to

www.ms.gov

and click on the Government tab. You can ask a parent, teacher, or librarian to help you find out which district you live in and how to contact your representatives to the US Congress.

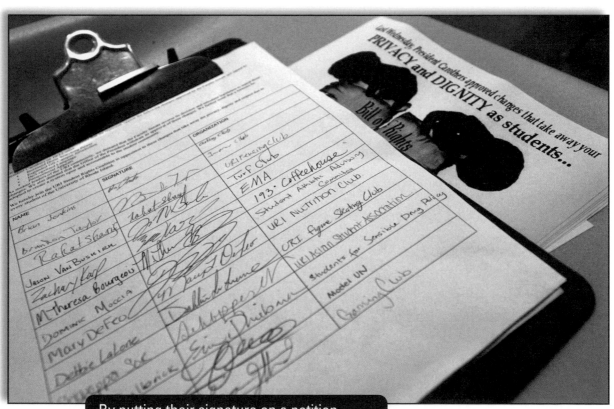

By putting their signature on a petition, people can let politicians know what issues are important to them.

Making a Living

For hundreds of years, most of Mississippi's wealth came from cotton growing. In fact, cotton made Mississippi one of the richest states in the Union 150 years ago. Today, profits from cotton growing make up a much smaller share of Mississippi's income.

In the years between the end of the Civil War and the beginning of World War II, many people in the state struggled to support themselves, as there were few high-paying jobs. Today, however, the situation has changed. The state government and private citizens have made successful efforts to attract new industries to Mississippi.

As in other parts of the United States, most people find employment in the service sector. That means they might work in banks or business offices, for example. Professional service jobs include those held by doctors, nurses, and lawyers. Tens of thousands of other people in the state hold some kind of government job, working for the federal, state, or local government. These people teach, govern, or work in state agencies—some as social workers, administrators, and managers, for example. Tourism is a major industry that creates many other kinds of service jobs in hotels, restaurants, casinos, and major tourists sites. Other workers manufacture goods in Mississippi's factories.

Farmers have been growing cotton in Mississippi's rich soil for centuries.

Mississippi's Industries and Workers (May 2013)

Industry	Number of People Working in That Industry	Percentage of Labor Force Working in That Industry
Farming	71,000	5.9%
Mining and Logging	9,400	0.8%
Construction	51,900	4.3%
Manufacturing	134,800	11.3%
Trade, Transportation, and Utilities	216,800	18.2%
Information	12,400	1%
Professional & Business Services	105,200	8.8%
Education & Health Services	135,200	11.3%
Leisure & Hospitality	125,500	10.5%
Government	249,400	20.9%
Other Services	36,900	3.1%
Totals	**467,674**	**100%**

Notes: Figures above do not include people in the armed forces.
"Professionals" includes people such as doctors and lawyers.

Source: U.S. Bureau of Labor Statistics

Agriculture

In some periods, such as the time before the Civil War, Mississippi supported vast farmlands that made some people wealthy. Then war, social changes such as the end of slavery, and agricultural competition altered Mississippi's farm economy. Some Mississippians who grew food and cash crops hit difficult times.

In 1929, the Great Depression began. During this period, the national economy collapsed. Mississippi remained a farming state, but a poor one. In 1936, the state government made an effort to change the nature of the state's economy. It created a new program called Balance Agriculture with Industry. In the years that followed, more and more factories opened across the state. These included furniture and clothing manufacturers that could take advantage of Mississippi's lumber and cotton industries.

Today the people of Mississippi make their living in a variety of ways. Agriculture remains the state's most important economic base. Cotton, which is used to make cloth, is the third largest crop in Mississippi with nearly 600 million dollars in revenue each year. Cottonseeds can also be crushed to make oil and shortening that are used in food processing. Cottonseed feed is used for livestock.

Although cotton remains a major crop, farmers also grow different kinds of crops. Beginning around the 1930s, they began to produce large amounts of soybeans, for example, and crops used for livestock feed. Today, Mississippi has become known for its sweet potatoes, as well as for its pecans, which grow in the state's many orchards.

Other major crops include rice, hay, wheat, and corn. Livestock and livestock products contribute to Mississippi's yearly farm income. Chickens and beef cattle are the state's most valuable livestock. Mississippi usually ranks among the top five states in producing chickens, called broilers. Farmers also sell large numbers of hogs and chicken eggs as well as substantial amounts of dairy products.

RECIPE FOR SWEET AND SPICY PECANS

Pecan trees grew in the wild long before people came to the southern part of North America. These nutritious nuts were an important part of the diets of Native American and European settlers. Later, settlers began to cultivate, or grow, pecan trees as a cash crop. Today, Mississippi growers produce about 6.5 million pounds (2.9 million kg) of pecans each year. The nuts are a delicious ingredient in pies, vegetable and meat dishes, candies, and snacks.

INGREDIENTS

2 cups pecan halves

2 tablespoons melted butter in a bowl

1/2 teaspoon of hot sauce

1 tablespoon sugar

1/2 teaspoon chili powder

1/2 teaspoon ground cumin

Small pinch of salt

Have an adult help you preheat the oven to 325°F (163°C).

Line a baking sheet with foil and set it aside while you prepare the pecans.

Coat the pecans with the melted butter and hot sauce. Combine the remaining dry ingredients in a bowl. Pour the dry ingredients over the pecans to coat them.

Spread the pecans on the baking sheet in a single layer. Bake the pecans for 15 minutes, turning the pecans over at least once. (Have an adult help you with this since the baking sheet and the nuts will be hot!)

Remove the baking sheet from the oven. Wait for the pecans to cool for about 10 minutes, then nibble on this Mississippi treat!

Fishing

Taking advantage of their state's abundant inland waters, many Mississippians make their money from catfish farms. Mississippi leads all states in the production of freshwater catfish on farms. Mississippians also fish the state's rivers and lakes and harvest shrimp and oysters off the state's southern coast. Pascagoula-Moss Point is one of the nation's leading fishing ports. Biloxi is the state's chief shrimp port.

Lumbering

Thanks to its extensive forests, Mississippi typically ranks among the ten leading states that produce forestry products. Mississippi farmers grow some of the nation's Christmas trees. Forest products also include pine and hardwood lumber as well as pulpwood that is used to make paper. The state's superior lumber has led to the development of factories that make furniture and other wood products. Over two hundred furniture companies in the northeastern corner of Mississippi produce furniture from local lumber cut in the state's sawmills. Since the early 1990s, many of the new jobs in the state were in the furniture and wood products industry.

Inland waterways, as well as Mississippi's Gulf Coast, support a thriving fishing economy in the state.

Mississippi's furniture makers and wood carvers stay close to their state's extensive forests to produce their goods.

Manufacturing

Mississippi not only grows cotton, but its textile mills and clothing manufacturers turn that cotton into fabric and clothing right in the state. Other Mississippi factories produce packaged foods, paint, transportation equipment, and electronic equipment. More than 6,000 people work in Mississippi's chemical industry. Some of the chemicals are made from state's oil and mineral resources.

Workers in some of Mississippi's factories produce aerospace equipment and motor vehicle parts. Factories in Tupelo, Columbus, Jackson, and Natchez produce wood products. Corinth and Jackson are the chief centers for producing electronic equipment. Meatpacking, poultry processing, the manufacturing of cheese, and the canning and freezing of fish are important food industries. Other items manufactured in Mississippi include industrial machinery, chemicals, fabricated metal products, and refined petroleum. Today the state is a leader in the telecommunications industry, with over 300,000 miles (482,803 km) of fiber optic cables placed in the ground.

Oil and Gas

In the twentieth century, Mississippians found a new way to make money when oil was discovered for the first time in Yazoo County. The first oil well produced oil in

1939. Today there are several thousand wells that produce millions of barrels of oil each year. The state also produces a great deal of the country's natural gas.

Other materials mined in Mississippi include sand, gravel, crushed stone, and limestone, as well as clay, marl, cement rock, sandstone, bentonite, and fuller's earth, a kind of clay used in processing certain oils.

New Horizons

For a long time, Mississippi's economy was slow to grow. Over the last several decades, though, the state's leaders have worked hard to change that. One way they have done so is to attract tourists and retired people to their state. Each year, several million travelers come to Mississippi to enjoy its natural beauty and warm weather. While visiting, they spend money by staying in hotels and motels, buying gas for their cars, and eating out at restaurants. The annual economic benefit of tourism to the state is nearly $6 billion.

The Navy brought the USS *Cole*, which was damaged by a terrorist attack in 2000, to Ingalls Shipbuilding, in Pascagoula, for repairs.

Products & Resources

Catfish

Mississippi has more catfish than any other state. Beginning in the 1960s, many farmers, whose land had been overused for cotton growing, decided to try something new. They began to dig ponds for raising catfish. Today the state exports millions of pounds (kg) of the fish every year.

Chickens

In the 1940s, Mississippi farmers started to raise chickens on a large scale. Today the state has about 2,000 poultry farms producing 757 million broilers each year. Mississippi is also home to the largest egg processing company in the world.

Cotton

Cotton is still a major industry in Mississippi, with more than 1 million acres (405,000 ha) planted each year. Cotton plants yield cotton bolls, which are picked and then pulled apart to make thread that can then be woven into fabric.

Oil and Gas

A long time ago, seas covered all of Mississippi. When the water receded, rich deposits of petroleum and minerals were left behind. In 1939, the news broke that an oil well in Yazoo County had begun to produce. By 1970, the state's wells numbered in the thousands, which together yielded more than 65 million barrels of oil every year. Another of the state's natural resources is natural gas, which can be used to generate electricity. Mississippi has hundreds of oil and gas fields and is one of the top 15 oil producing states.

Soybeans

Soybeans have become one of Mississippi's biggest crops in recent years. About 1.8 million acres (728,000 ha) are planted each year, bringing in around $860 million in production value. Soybeans are a major ingredient in livestock feed. They can also be made into products such as tofu, soy milk, and soybean oil.

Sweet Potatoes

In northern Mississippi, farmers plant about 20,000 acres (8,094 ha) of sweet potatoes each year. Everyone agrees that sweet potatoes grown in the rich soils of northern Mississippi are especially good. Their sales bring close to $82 million into the state economy every year.

Many visitors travel along the Natchez Trace Parkway, which follows the route of the Natchez Trace, an important road in the history of Mississippi and the South that connects Natchez and Nashville, Tennessee. Other National Park Service areas in the state are Brices Cross Roads National Battlefield Site near Tupelo, Gulf Islands National Seashore, Tupelo National Battlefield, and Vicksburg National Military Park.

Looking to the Future

Almost every Mississippi industry was affected in some way by Hurricane Katrina in 2005, and it has taken several years for the state to fully recover. Mississippi received another blow in 2010 when the *Deepwater Horizon* oil rig exploded in the Gulf of Mexico. For nearly three months, oil gushed into the Gulf and made its way to the state's beaches. Marine life in the Gulf was damaged and the state's tourism industry suffered. Once again, though, the people of Mississippi came together to do all they could to protect their state. Today, tourists and Mississippians alike can once again enjoy the state's beautiful beaches and wildlife.

Mississippians have endured many hard times. However, they continue to rebuild their state with determination and strength. They are committed to making their state better than ever!

State Flag & Seal

The Mississippi flag, adopted in 1894, has a square in the corner with thirteen stars. These are said to represent the thirteen original colonies of the United States. During the period when the South formed the Confederate States of America, the stars represented the thirteen southern states in the Confederacy. The three equal bars are blue, white, and red.

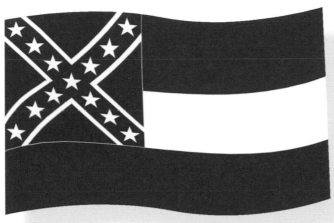

In the center of Mississippi's state seal is an eagle. Across its chest lies a shield, with stars at the top and stripes down below. The eagle, with widespread wings, clasps both an olive branch and arrows in its talons. This symbolizes that the state desires peace but is prepared to fight.

Mississippi State Map

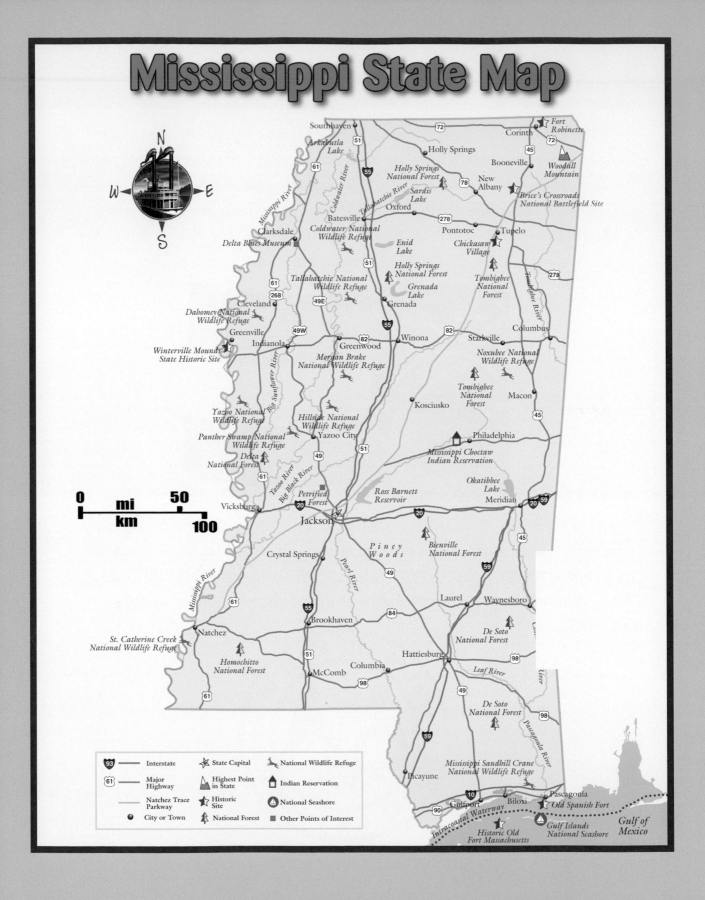

N
W E
S

Southhaven
Arkabutla Lake
51
61
Coldwater River
Holly Springs
55
72
Fort Robinette
Corinth
45
72
Booneville
New Albany
78
Woodall Mountain
Brice's Crossroads National Battlefield Site
Holly Springs National Forest
Sardis Lake
Oxford
Tallahatchie River
Batesville
278
Pontotoc
Tupelo
278
Clarksdale
Delta Blues Museum
Coldwater National Wildlife Refuge
Enid Lake
Chickasaw Village
61
268
Holly Springs National Forest
Grenada Lake
Grenada
Tombigbee National Forest
Tombigbee River
Cleveland
49E
Tallahatchie National Wildlife Refuge
Winona
82
Starkville
Columbus
82
Dahomey National Wildlife Refuge
49W
55
Noxubee National Wildlife Refuge
Greenville
Indianola
Greenwood
Winterville Mounds State Historic Site
Morgan Brake National Wildlife Refuge
Big Sunflower River
Kosciusko
Tombigbee National Forest
Macon
45
Yazoo National Wildlife Refuge
Hillside National Wildlife Refuge
Philadelphia
Panther Swamp National Wildlife Refuge
Yazoo City
51
Mississippi Choctaw Indian Reservation
Delta National Forest
49
Yazoo River
Big Black River
Okatibbee Lake
0   mi   50
km
100
Vicksburg
20
Petrified Forest
Ross Barnett Reservoir
20
Meridian
20
59
Jackson
45
Piney Woods
Bienville National Forest
Crystal Springs
59
Mississippi River
Pearl River
49
61
Laurel
Waynesboro
55
84
Brookhaven
De Soto National Forest
98
St. Catherine Creek National Wildlife Refuge
Natchez
51
Hattiesburg
Leaf River
98
Homochitto National Forest
Columbia
49
McComb
98
De Soto National Forest
61
98
Pascagoula River
59
Mississippi Sandhill Crane National Wildlife Refuge
Picayune
10
Pascagoula
Old Spanish Fort
90
Gulfport
Biloxi
Intracoastal Waterway
Historic Old Fort Massachusetts
Gulf Islands National Seashore
Gulf of Mexico

93 — Interstate
61 — Major Highway
Natchez Trace Parkway
City or Town
State Capital
Highest Point in State
Historic Site
National Forest
National Wildlife Refuge
Indian Reservation
National Seashore
Other Points of Interest

State Song

Go, Mississippi!

words and music by William Houston Davis

States may sing their songs of praise, With wav - ing flags and hip - hoo - rays, Let

cym - bals crash and let bells ring 'Cause here's one song I'm proud to sing.

CHORUS

GO, MIS - SIS - SIP - PI, keep roll - ing a - long, ___

GO, MIS - SIS - SIP - PI, you can - not go wrong, ___

GO, MIS - SIS - SIP - PI, we're sing - ing your song, ___

M - I - S - S - I - S - S - I - P - P - I.

BOOKS

Johnson, Robin. *The Mississippi: America's Mighty River.* Rivers Around the World. New York: Crabtree Publishing, 2010.

Nelson, Robin. *From Cotton to T-Shirt.* Start to Finish: Everyday Products. Minneapolis, MN: Lerner Classroom, 2013.

Somervill, Barbara. *Mississippi.* From Sea to Shining Sea. Danbury, CT: Children's Press, 2009.

WEBSITES

Mississippi History Now, an online publication of the Mississippi Historical Society
http://mshistory.k12.ms.us

Mississippi Museum of Natural Science
www.mdwfp.com/museum.aspx

Official State Website of Mississippi
www.ms.gov

Ann Graham Gaines is a freelance author who lives with her children in a cabin in the woods near Gonzales, Texas.